ROUGH FIRE

poems by

Ronald Dzerigian

Finishing Line Press
Georgetown, Kentucky

ROUGH FIRE

Copyright © 2018 by Ronald Dzerigian
ISBN 978-1-63534-610-7 First Edition
All rights reserved under International and Pan-American Copyright Conventions.
No part of this book may be reproduced in any manner whatsoever without written permission from the publisher, except in the case of brief quotations embodied in critical articles and reviews.

ACKNOWLEDGMENTS

I would like to thank my wife, Ariela, for being the most candid first reader a poet could ever hope to have, and our daughters, Gabriela and Faith, for their unyielding support and patience. I offer additional gratitude to Mike Cole, who introduced me to poetry from California's Central Valley, and to Corrinne Clegg Hales and Tim Skeen, who taught me excavation and risk. Also, my thanks to the editors of print and online journals—and the one anthology—in which versions of the following poems first appeared.

The Academy of American Poets (poets.org), 2015: "Our California"
A Sharp Piece of Awesome, 2017: "My Grandfather Gives Me Advice in a Dream" and "The Paperboy"
Australian Book Review, March 2017: "Four Egrets" (shortlisted for the Peter Porter Poetry Prize)
The Biggest Valley: Poems from California's Heartland, 2018: "Coyote, Fog, West on Highway 43," "Exit West Through the Gates of Stanislaus County," and "The River Witch"
Crosswinds Poetry Journal, 2016: "Small Prayer: South-West Fresno County"
F(r)ictionOnline, 2016: "Contemplating the First and Last Crops of M. Theo Kearney"
The Gordian Review, 2016: "The Long Way to Fresno" and "Too Many Crows in Clovis, CA"
HyeBred Magazine, 2017: "Portrait of a Poem in Summer"
Prairie Schooner, 2016-2017: "This Side of Paradise," "Bathing my Grandfather," and "To a Possible Tenant"
RHINO, 2017: "Dream of Light and Space Debris"
The San Joaquin Review, 2015: "Hardpan"
Salamander, 2017: "Our School Colors"
Santa Ana River Review, 2015: "Anthony, Class of '92, On a Sunday Morning" and "Brothers Walk the Old Farm in a Dream"
3 Elements Literary Review, 2016: "Measured by the Opening of a Door"
Watershed Review, 2016: "Chopping Wood to Build a House" and "Two Brothers in the Woods When the Bees Have Left"

Publisher: Leah Maines
Editor: Christen Kincaid
Cover Art: Steve Dzerigian
Author Photo: Ariela Dzerigian
Cover Design: Ronald Dzerigian

Printed in the USA on acid-free paper.
Order online: www.finishinglinepress.com
also available on amazon.com

Author inquiries and mail orders:
Finishing Line Press
P. O. Box 1626
Georgetown, Kentucky 40324
U. S. A.

Table of Contents

MY GRANDFATHER GIVES ME ADVICE IN A DREAM

I.

FOUR EGRETS 1
ROUGH FIRE 3
DIRECTIONS THROUGH SMOKE 4
THE LONG WAY TO FRESNO 5
TWO BROTHERS IN THE WOODS WHEN THE
    BEES HAVE LEFT 6
DESERTER SONGS FOR BOB RAFELSON 7
MONTEREY, 1987 8
PUTTING OUR ANIMALS TO SLEEP 10
SUNDAY RIVER RAFTING IN THE EYES OF GOD 11
SMALL PRAYER: SOUTH-WEST FRESNO COUNTY 12

II.

TO A POSSIBLE TENANT 15
A LESSON 16
TO A CHILD IN DREAMTIME 17
WILDIE 18
AFTER THE WHALE 19
DROUGHT 20
RED 21
SUMMER DIVES 22
WHILE PLAYING PICKLEBALL ALONE 23
THIS SIDE OF PARADISE 24

III.

SONG TO THE SON OF A JOURNEYMAN 27
CHOPPING WOOD TO BUILD A HOUSE 28
BROTHERS WALK THE OLD FARM IN A DREAM 29
COYOTE, FOG, WEST ON HIGHWAY 43 30
THE TRAIN AND ORION 31
EXIT WEST THROUGH THE GATES OF
    STANISLAUS COUNTY 32

AFTER VISITING THE CEMETERY AT ACADEMY, CA 33
ATTEMPTING SLEEP IN A JANUARY LAKE HOUSE 34
MEASURED BY THE OPENING OF A DOOR 35
THE PAPERBOY 36
FOR PEOPLE WHO FLY 37
AN EASTER GIFT 38
FOLLOWING A BIRD 39
OUR CALIFORNIA 40

IV.

BATHING MY GRANDFATHER 43
RETRIEVING POMEGRANATES 44
DREAM OF LIGHT AND SPACE DEBRIS 45
CONTEMPLATING THE FIRST AND LAST CROPS OF
    M. THEO KEARNEY 47
ANTHONY, CLASS OF '92, ON A SUNDAY MORNING 48
OUR SCHOOL COLORS 49
THE RIVER WITCH 51
RIDE THE 28 ACROSS THE RIVER STYX 53
LISTENING TO NINA SIMONE SING SINNERMAN 54
HARDPAN 55

V.

PORTRAIT OF A POEM IN SUMMER 59
CORAL SCRAPES HIS BACK 60
THOUGH THE EARTH BE MOVED 61
FOUND PHOTO FROM A GRADUATION 62
ON THURSDAY MORNING, THE ROAD WAKES 63
SUMMER ENDS EACH MORNING 64
PROUD FLESH 65
WE NAME THE FOX 66
SOMETHING IN THE WALL 67
THE CARBON FOOTPRINT OF A RATTLESNAKE 68
LOGIC 69
WAKING TO WATCH ACCIDENTS ON YOUTUBE 70
TOO MANY CROWS IN CLOVIS, CA 71
DEER AND SNOW IN LAKEVIEW, OR 73

for my family

MY GRANDFATHER GIVES ME ADVICE IN A DREAM

*Take a teaspoon of dirt
sift it through the eye
of a peacock feather.
Purify
the radiated earth.*

*Take three tiny ears
of dried apricot.
Name them Grit, Levity,
Science. Eat them and follow
with a tall glass of milk.*

*Take eight pretzel sticks,
break them into varying lengths,
crush them.
Add water, shape an infant
from the salty dough.*

I.

FOUR EGRETS

Four white egrets perch on four baby citrus trees
at the four corners of the world and you wouldn't

see this if you were not told to look. Their black
eyes stare at the drying canal and stave hunger

for snail and frog and minnow, because those remains
are not more than sinew or bone in cracking mud.

The two llamas and two horses in the chain-linked
front yard, the one tree in that yard that has been

stripped of bark and leaves, the four of them eating
hay that has been spread across cement—you would

not share their thirst at the moment you hope
for rain to fall on your dusty truck because you see

them everyday and their backs are not your dusty
truck. You wouldn't see the barn buried under piles

of hardwood vine stakes or wonder what is inside
the barn in the no-light—you would not, before

it's gone. And what about the distribution of bee
corpses from your wind-shield into fine dust under

the few wilted melons near goathead thorns? The hard
and tiny horns may stick to your boot and you must

shake them loose after stepping back into the truck
after taking a picture of the patch of weeds near sun-

bleached powder that streams across the upward face
of the asphaltic chipseal—and further out, you may

see the glint of shimmering mylar balloons that
have released their helium and have set themselves

softly down, like dropped testicles, displaying bright
round words that announce *happy birthday* or *over*

the hill and you would not remember what day
it was when you decided to try to be someone else

between shifts, between each appearance of your-
self embedded in the structures of everything but you.

ROUGH FIRE

Dry weeds spark. Logs, red-brown blue-oaks, mice, squirrel, hog,
all fold into flame. A mountain lion at the pool behind a tract home

startles an elderly woman into throes of cardiac arrest. After swarms
of hummingbirds leave feeders dry, after the buckeye has dropped

its fruit, after my hands close the book and I drain the water bottle,
the wind-chime-song rises again with meat-bees coveting the un-tended

bowl of dog food. The sun dries the fluids, preserves the meat. Maybe
that is it—the thing turkey vultures circle, this August, as the hills ignite.

DIRECTIONS THROUGH SMOKE

When headed toward the mountains
invisible in the distance—

past the *world's best
hamburgers and Chinese food,*

past the tiny CVS pharmacy, past
the Ace Hardware gift shop, past

abandoned newspaper offices,
past *need to read a good book? /*

come on in / we use the best seller
on the Baptist church marquee,

past the amphitheater
where local ne'er-do-wells hang

while eating Takis Fuego, smoking
cigarettes—stop near the tallest

yellow light in the one city park
that makes glow the line

of chain linked backyards.
Stop at the falling pinecones,

too dry and small to seed. Stop
at the whimper of swings.

THE LONG WAY TO FRESNO

If a small plane crashes into a swimming pool early
in the morning, will the burst of water and flame rise
up in slow motion and snuff immediately out? Will leaf

shift out of socket and fall? This is what I think about
while driving the 58 N.W. toward Tehachapi, the long
way to Fresno, on purpose. The radio drops out; the few

gas stations are unpopulated. Rusty Ford pickup, '50s,
fenced into a dry pasture, poses—storied—with a dust
devil. I am thirty-six, transitioning from a marriage;

I'm happy on the road and I don't have to go
where I am going. I see air flex against the small wings
of a barn swallow; I conjure metal folding around

the young pilot's head, a pillow, a chlorine lullaby, gasoline,
a mixture for sipping at the gate. When I was five or six,
sitting near my father as he drove the road from Dunlap

to Fresno, I would imagine having wings, tracing my toes
along the Kings River's crests and furrows; I see my body
above the fields' waves of heat and breath of raisins.

TWO BROTHERS IN THE WOODS WHEN THE BEES HAVE LEFT

for Jake

We dig our hands into the fallen pine,
wet, moss-covered and cobwebbed; the pieces
fall apart. The pearl-yellow termites pour
out. Legs that seem supple and translucent
in the timber-scattered light carry their
tracks across our forearms. We shake them off
like almond blossoms.

                        We dig, gather pulp
beneath fingernails. My brother pulls back
a shield of bark. A knot unplugs the damp
black; gold bleeds out. Our palms cup the honey.
Floating wax sinks and turns in the shallow
amber we bring to our lips. The crickets
go silent, the pines stand still, and we drink.

DESERTER SONGS FOR BOB RAFELSON

I.

Stand and watch water gather in the gutter. Watch it collect papers, leaves, oil. Watch it deepen, sculpt mountain ranges out of dirt, wash them away.

II.

Feel the pull of the sea. Tide pools hide when spotted by the sun. The breeze touches the stillness of this bench and, yes, the stillness can break any thing.

III.

Drive. Rain slips across the glass as light cuts lines from telephone poles. Drive. Hear trees sing hymns through sheets of mist. They are clear green.

IV.

Walk along the sand bank. Look at wet-white squares on the walls of canals. Weigh beachfront cities. Take bends from the arms of highways.

MONTEREY, 1987

In the tiny house, snowed in, pox and fever
introduce me to Jacques Cousteau. My blood
becomes the sea, my heart the red cap.

In mid-January, the fog lifts and I am anxious
to build a dam around my feet. I walk away
from Ricketts' lab. I am no longer a child.

Shoes off, I travel between the anemones
in the tide pools. I no longer know the smells
of my father's Volkswagen bus, my stepfather's

Dodge Ram. My bedroom above Hume Lake
comes back as pine needles, snow drifts.
I remember the touch of typha against my thin

white shoulder. A circle of coyotes call across
the surface of frozen Hume. The moon is white
as salt. I reach down, touch a barnacle. The water

does not recede—the dam has sprung a leak—
my hair is algae. I ask to hear it again, the poem
sung by my mother as the sun purples up. *Red sky*

at night, sailor's delight / red sky in the morning,
sailor's warning. The rain has arrived, wrinkling
the clouds. I come here to hear you, mother/father/

stepfather/stepmother. The tide is quick to bring
you to me—tentacles retreat when I try to touch.
The coyotes inherit; the ice will never be the same.

I break a piece of stone, pitch it out. My sleeves
are wet. The aquariums are broken, gray, eclipsed.
I still have three craters on my forehead—

what's gone stays. Thin strands of sea grass curl out
of a beer bottle. The sand crab is eating; the urchin
is not snowed in. Winter does not last forever.

Pinecones fall at night—the only sounds other
than my breathing. These sounds disappear—
the sounds of escape.

PUTTING OUR ANIMALS TO SLEEP

for Matt

I ask you to remember that you were a child.
Remember the dead parakeet in the blue heat of summer.

Remember how you swallowed perfumes, the hospital; how
you threatened to sail from the U.S. to New Zealand alone.

You knew that idea would haunt us like the turn of a blade
once it's entered a body. Remember, brother, the rooms

you've lived in, the people that circle you, the animals
you've fed, your dreams before falling into deep sleep;

look across dinner tables. Think of family trips in the orange
and white Volkswagen bus. Remember the western states;

how we watched *Highway to Heaven* in motel rooms, roved
Anasazi ruins, expressed raw pleasure when a motel had a pool,

recited: *coffee, donuts, soda-pop, cigarettes, gasoline, beer.*
We stared out windows, took pictures with our Instamatics:

us, our sisters, landscape, buildings, animals, the road. Do not
forget the homes we visited, in the woods, by rivers, in cities.

Remember the pets, the air, your father gone. Think about quiet
cassettes, mute road games, little black eyes closed.

SUNDAY RIVER RAFTING IN THE EYES OF GOD

We've taken the rafts to the river and put the beer
on ice. I am floating near the others but fall beneath

the surface to see if I can disappear. I cannot see
their lower halves and I shouldn't have opened

my eyes in the mineral-thick deep brown green.
The light is above me and I can hear their voices;

they do not yet know that in one year's time, I will
have omitted them from my life. I take a drag

from a cigarette and regret the act of smoking, the act
of borrowing smoke. I go under. The river, the warm

Pabst, mud between limbs, swarms of mosquito.
I am a child in the water, drowning and not drowning,

ending it and not ending anything. I am a coward
amongst cowards as we secretly urinate into the cold

snowmelt. It's odd, the juvenile effort to lengthen
the reckless stay. I should be several years closer

to retirement or just leaving church services
with my children and wife by my side—a man no

longer young. Water-plant debris, agricultural runoff,
mud from deer hoof and bear paw, fish scale, barbed

wire rust, squirrel corpse—a percentage of all this
works into my skull, through tear duct and nostril—

becomes part of me. *There are no regrets*, says
a lousy friend, but I choose to spell out my regret—

finally—letter by letter, slowly, assuredly, counting
each raft's wake to draft them, at last, in past tense.

SMALL PRAYER: SOUTH-WEST FRESNO COUNTY

beginning with a line from Weldon Kees' Small Prayer

Change, move, dead clock, that this fresh day may break.
I picture myself waking
in the cornhusker's state, roots unveiled, soil rinsed.
Yet I stop at the corner of East Nebraska
and South Fowler Avenues, listen to
the engine hum. From this place, escape routes

look clear. No need to call home. No need
to turn; no need to go. A eucalyptus
explodes with sparrows and a thin branch floats
down. Vineyard sinks and wilts upon its stakes.
A man stands at his fence, dog leashed, looks at

the sky. This is a slow motion place, where
morning comes and comes. Dusk and morning join
and disjoin constantly. A man could leave
keys in the ignition here, could vanish,
traceless. Nebraska calls. I breathe in the
California pheromone. Mute the call.

II.

TO A POSSIBLE TENANT

    for Ariela

I have polished the old wood floors for you,
        covered the oak with three coats of lacquer

so you can see yourself when you look down.
        I've replaced the tile using good strong grout

that will not crumble for at least one life-
        time. All of the boxes that sat, browning

in the garage, have been thrown out. The walls,
        white, wait for your white car to fill the space

with infinite comings and goings. New
        sink for the kitchen, plain weave curtains, new

stove. The ceiling no longer holds on to
        the past. The rooms are empty and I stand

in them daily, counting filled cracks, minutes,
        the new pictures to be hung on our walls.

A LESSON

Cut white apple
        meat from paper.

Glue red skin, stems,
        to each body.

Small fingers hold
        scissors, carefully.

Remains speck the milk-
        white tile.

Petals separate
        from their branches.

Not bitten, never to grow,
        rot, or be eaten.

These blooms repeat
        their unfolding.

TO A CHILD IN DREAMTIME

To the child playing in the green,
who pities and allows larva to cocoon.

To the five-spotted hawkmoth, once
a gorged and pure scented tomato horn-

worm—who emerges, no longer
of full meaty body—who persists slow,

and enormous, for those who fear
her powdery span. To those wings, push

lazy wind aside. Her dust belongs
to earth. Watch from windows. Dream

of a time when you were the moth; see
the lake's obsidian surface open up.

WILDIE

> It is rumored that filmmaker Hal Roach would employ someone who, often drunk or crazy, would be called upon during the writing process to come up with an outlandish plot twist.

The city wraps itself so tight it swallows lost cars.
I take this from a poem I wrote on our wedding night:

Valentine's Day, 2015, the day Philip
Levine died. *John Coltrane Plays the Blues* is on the record

player. Light from the Oliver Hardy lamp behind
our bed casts deep shadows from the corners of our bookshelves

down the legs of our queen. Pendleton wool cocoons us;
the dog is in there too and we hear "Mr. Day" finish.

No kisses needed, cold hands held, no insulation
in this old apartment to keep the neighbor's voices out.

I picture Stan and Ollie on a flimsy bridge
between two cliffs in the Swiss Alps; there is a gorilla

in the cottage on the other side. I hear nothing,
no questions asked when cancer takes, when a wedding creates

a family, when 4:00 a.m. mist wets and muffles
tires in February. Coltrane's liver cancer took him in '67.

My wife looks up the word *heath*—we talk about rabbits
beneath the low shrubs, their small bodies stolen by hawks.

AFTER THE WHALE

for Jane Kenyon and Donald Hall

In the morning, breach, wake with cattle, stack
        hay. Hands raw from pitchfork-handle pool milk,

skim cream, lay to rest heavy eyes when it
        is time. Nothing stays. Cow paths meander

with the seasons; barn inches toward the pond
        with each rain. Soon the milk will snake paths

as sea-brine returns hoof to fin. The farm
        will return to soil, as all things do; the cock

will sound his depth charge. But, for now,
        we watch numbers wane in National

Geographic magazine and understand
        that after the whale succumbs to Ahab,

as beef to knife, as we inherit
        the earth, the sea will inherit us.

DROUGHT

    for Ariela

I can see myself washing dishes, red dusk under
the window, the cloud, the full shadow of the red-

tailed hawk that holds the last muscle flex of a gopher
snake. The coyote that took the dog died long ago

from starvation; its ghost-speak can be heard
along the cemented stone banks of the dry creek bed.

In the beds where we sleep, stories gather.
Coyote house echo phantom yelp, vineyard song.

We can never know the songs of the neighboring
trees, never know the poems written on their bark.

The home is there for us in dreams only; coyote ghosts
gather at the border between yellow and blue. Hills cut

the sky apart; the hunters of the sky halt. We dream
of floor, of roof, of stone wall bite, stone wall shelter.

Let us place the salt lick in the corner of our lot,
barn the horse, drink from the well while we can.

Give us the stonemason's gift, we ask in quiet,
as we plan trips for our children. Without driving,

we are already traveling; the mounds of peat moss,
dried and hard, pull from the granite, the brown-

red soil, the dirt cracks under feet. We will lay
our foundation. One bedroom here, another there.

RED

I grew up with animals, wild
and otherwise. The open

mouth of any hungry thing
is red. A helmeted curassow

bites the finger of a child
at the zoo, her father pulls

back, tells her, *don't be afraid
of the unexpected.* My old Radio

Flyer lays overturned in the dirt,
belly-up, wheels reeling. My niece

has used it to bound over
driveway gravel, as I once did.

SUMMER DIVES

This straw hat smells of tamarind; the pool shimmers with the shock
of my daughters' dives. They do not know the delicate strands I hold
tightly to keep them. The carol of sparrow stops while big sister offers

advice on how to avoid belly flops. A church rings out. Summer storm
lights up the lines where houses meet sky. Water gathers in the cement
cracks, makes dams and lakes for all the tiny things crawling around

our feet. No matter how big we get, the little things stay small. I see
a man walking with his mother, they talk intently; I imagine eighty-year-
old gossip: this woman lost her dog, the young man who played hopscotch

gone missing, the house for sale on the corner where an old boyfriend
lived. Sparks travel the outlines of clouds. My hat soaks a drop of rain;
the dust upon *remate* sweat and hay-bail heat carries a tropical musk. The

swims into parent's arms, ants, elder fugues, walks through memory
wires all tangled in water, electricity, the hunger of departures. Walk me,
children, around a block in forty years, listen to recollections disperse.

WHILE PLAYING PICKLEBALL ALONE

Dull pings, plastic, hollow pings, pops, not thuds,
not thick skinned, not thin; a medium sound. Equate

this sound to cello—closest to the human voice: Pablo
Cassals, Beatrice Harrison, Concerto in B Minor,

B. 191 (Op. 104) by Anton Dvorak. Note the bright
green aluminum plaque that states the rules, the wood

paddle, the green ball, the perforation. Note elbow
sinew, the frequent gulps from the $14.99 Nalgene

water bottle; note the music, a shift in physiology.
Decorate a shirt with medals for each year lived. Play

retiree, RV owner, grandparent, will-and-testament
reviser, mall-walker after a youth long-lived. Now,

dismiss the music festivals, the artisan beers; dismiss
lunches at the bar, black-hole trips to spend student

loans; dismiss skateboards and fold-up scooters, dismiss
internet, flu-shots; dismiss methane fumes of dairy

manure management programs, trees drained of water;
dismiss children trading candy for kindle apps; dismiss

the president's baggy eyes, a bird with a broken wing
nestled to die inside a well-trimmed hedge at sundown.

THIS SIDE OF PARADISE

I fear memory loss, like anyone;
I fear sub-consciousness skipping out mid-

sentence. In conversation, I drift out
toward the oak tree that appeared in a poem

I wrote the previous week. It is there,
right in front of me, when I thought I had

only imagined it. A crow, open-
beaked, dry-tongued, shines, oil-slicked and hungry.

Will this memory recall itself later
while I try writing about my grandfather

awaiting chicken-fried-steak prepped for father's
day dinner in the Alzheimer's facility?

Maybe. Head tilt up in recognition,
then, recognition gone.

I want to hold my grandfather's face in
my hands, speak to him with words that cut-

out, blink-out; speak in the language of for-
getfulness. I fear cupping his cheek to

feel the shave escaped from morning rites; I
fear my own rituals gone one day. My

wife holding my face above the bathtub
water, eyes black as every part crow.

III.

SONG TO THE SON OF A JOURNEYMAN

Learn, child, to fold the quilt and make your bed before leaving
        the house. Find small troubles boring to discuss. Say, also,

that *only boring people get bored*. Then, sweet one, know
        that tying a shoe is first before finding one's way in this world;

leave keys under the mat as the bells of St. Therese chime
        through the branches of the bay tree. The oak at the corner

of the lot stops as the wind ceases, then the bay. One cannot
        loose another knot without losing control of the sail. Aim

home; take walks along bridges. One turn is slight;
        leaf can curl under the first May heat-wave.

CHOPPING WOOD TO BUILD A HOUSE

for Ariela

Honey, let us wet the backs of our shirts
        upon the lawn as we hear the branches move

against each other in this city, in the hum of carpenter
        bees inside our heads as we contemplate webs of dead

spiders and termite frass in the halls of the mid-century home
        we cannot afford, in classrooms of children, down deep

in the desire to make another, in university debts,
        janitorial jobs, in empty birdhouses and lava rock

paths, in the holes of trees as the humming
        continues to dig and dig and dig.

BROTHERS WALK THE OLD FARM IN A DREAM

for Jake

We two tramp our feet over seven acres
        of frozen cheatgrass and cracked drip line.

We carve our path, footing slick, ice
        melting into jackets. We can hear our blood—

weather-proof—oil in a hurricane lamp;
        our veins creeks that house cold minnows.

A view of dawn in the tropics: no. Only white—
        black soil revealed by stick when we write "two

boys in paradise," our names, as the sun rises
        over brittle tarweed warming under four boots.

COYOTE, FOG, WEST ON HIGHWAY 43

The coyote, there, the mother coyote
      is hungry; no hesitant

twitch from shifting rock will
      bring her to step

between two April cherry
      trees toward her pup

as the train shudders
      the gravel, as a jet

tries to open a foggy underbelly.
      No light, no blossom.

THE TRAIN AND ORION

No a/c. A daddy-long-leg's foot
        on my forehead. Moonlight, the roof,

one bad cigarette, a can of Budweiser.
        Trees thrash in hot wind. No rest

for the city that sings, *aww white heat*
        tickle me down to my toes. My virtue,

my *Franny and Zooey*, loaned,
        not returned. The train travels

Orion's path. Nighttime songbirds echo
        the slow gracelessness of junebug hiss.

EXIT WEST THROUGH THE GATES OF STANISLAUS COUNTY

Near Modesto, at sundown,
        a dog talks to crows. The crickets

click madly as the light goes
        out. The turn, ahead, whispers

the salt-air promise
        to wind-deaf boys

kicking leaves from the truck bed.
        They do not yet feel the spectral

night, the song
        of earthquakes.

AFTER VISITING THE CEMETERY AT ACADEMY, CA

for Philip Levine

It's dark beyond the shallow reach
      of my headlights. No crickets,

no little feet digging, no sound of breathing.
      The tall brown grasses

are unmoving, gray in this light.
      I know little about the bodies

under the earth, or who
      rests near their siblings.

One car passes,
      igniting a wall of trees.

ATTEMPTING SLEEP IN A JANUARY LAKE HOUSE

for Larry Levis

I wrap a canvas coat around my feet
        when ice lamina settles on my cheekbones,

when my shoulders fight the glacial night.
        Winter stars—all white—come in

at 4:00 a.m. above the lake to fill the space
        between trees. They bridge sleep to first light.

I feel the vacancy of color surrounding
        my fingers with hyperborean cotton. Images

of horses outside, draped in hard canvas,
        warm, blind, and cold.

MEASURED BY THE OPENING OF A DOOR

for Ariela

I stand at the door when it rains;
        the mug's hot face slivers

into the first blanket
        of finger skin. Ricochet of rain

cleaves and carries dirt, scatters it
        over my bare feet. The sky lights up;

I cannot predict each new strike. In stillness,
        I search. Our home still dark—my wife

walks to me. Each morning, with coffee,
        we—in turn—trade eyes.

THE PAPERBOY

Vartan serenaded Lucille;
        violin through the telephone.

Today they kiss,
        he at 93, her at 91,

and the plaque in his brain
        allows for one recitation—

Boston American only one cent,
        help my mother pay the rent.

He is singing,
        yet cannot say *Lucille.*

FOR PEOPLE WHO FLY

The fall is reported to me through NPR. How
        can the echo of one child falling 60 ft. from chalk edge

of white stone and blue—to his death on stone
        and sea shallows in Brighton—guide this man to rest

curbside? I have a fear of heights, not for myself,
        for others. I search my wife's face, hunger flight

from our ordinary throes. A featherless
        bird falls from a nest, swarms prematurely

with hungry ants while we wonder
        whether lightning will drop fire into oak.

AN EASTER GIFT

A young rabbit, mottled red pine
        brown, rested near the front door

during a quiet morning. I placed cilantro
        and spinach leaves near the hedge.

One or two days later, its limp body
        was pulled from the still apartment

complex swimming pool. When I swim
        I can see that small uncertain brain

that looked for water—sought exit
        from small Sunday hands.

FOLLOWING A BIRD

for Lucille

My wife and I drive to visit
        my grandmother near foothills in the low

sky of a season's final hot morning.
        A robin dives toward the windshield

from behind the car and looks back.
        The hills wave in the heat. The bird leads;

my foot presses a pedal that lets gas
        combust. My arm hairs live quietly

near my body—I'm near tears
        at each moment a mile disappears.

OUR CALIFORNIA

for Ariela

Backyards filled with pallets, piles
        of dry timber, pools unswimmed and dusty,

trailers parked in clusters of downy weeds.
        All of this is reflected in the freckle on the white

of your eye. Our fingers trace each other's fingers
        as we watch mockingbirds swoop after hawks.

We make our bed from eight hay bails
        so that we may sleep in vineyards stinking

of raisins. We collect our many beads
        of sweat and drink, smiling, by the river.

IV.

BATHING MY GRANDFATHER

I shave his face, careful to keep his moustache
just right, pencil-thin, the way grandmother likes,
undress him, help him into the shower. One
then two slow steps into the warm water. If
my hands are cold, he tells me. I place the white
bar of soap into the washcloth, start with his
feet, then his legs. My legs are his legs. When I
wash his penis I warn him, prepare him for
the discomfort. His testicles, feared damaged
from a fragment of factory pine, helped give
life to my father, helped me get to this bath-
room, this shower, this age. Every morning I
look into the mirror, naked. I see him: same
genitals, same thin frame, same misshapen chest.

RETRIEVING POMEGRANATES

for Edward Odd Lund III

The first day after you left,
while I drove along Fowler Avenue,
a cyclist paused, drinking water;

a farmer got out of his truck
to retrieve a few pomegranates
that had been displaced; an empty

wine bottle lay near the dry canal;
five puppies ran along the center
of the road, weaving across

the yellow line, weaving
in and out of sparse traffic;
I stopped to see them get to safety

and wanted to cry at this. I see you
everywhere now, waving to me.
I see you everywhere, displaced.

DREAM OF LIGHT AND SPACE DEBRIS

> *after reading* Searching for the International Space Station
> *by Sean Patrick Kinneen*

A stack of books, a ceramic walrus on top, a plant
—tips dry—in a white vase on a glass-topped burl

wood side table. My wife sleeps on the couch, feet
wrapped in a knitted throw; I watch her from

my chair. Her eyes turn beneath their lids; perhaps
her dreams consider the colors of light through blinds.

Our two girls sleep silently. Clock ticks; the ceiling
fan sounds like draining water. I've just read a poem

about a space station. It is moving; people are inside
turning knobs, eating, sleeping, weightless. A stack

of books would come apart in the heavens; light
is different without dust and rusted beams parting

plumes of atmosphere. Sleep pulls us through clouds
of memory—we forget who we are when we sleep.

Our youngest wakes us and we don't ask her to recall
the bad dream; it will be forgotten. My wife's face

moves against soft folds of woven pink, brown,
yellow, orange, waking without waking. The ceiling

fan sounds like water; the station remains above us;
our stack of books will not come apart mid-air.

I see the photograph of the one person bruised
by a meteorite, Ann Hodges—Sylacauga, Alabama—

struck in 1954 while napping on her couch. I think
of flames that rise from surfaces that cut across the sky,

lines ignited red or green. I consider the inability
to fall; the orbit of bodies that shine back as we look up.

CONTEMPLATING THE FIRST AND LAST CROPS OF M. THEO KEARNEY

Listen to desert sounds give; till for grape.
The morning basin hums as a drip traps
a fragment of sun and converts it. A
stir of dirt, silk-fine, may destroy a mass
of ants, soundlessly. What water level
is needed to fill porous stone, to give

at shovel entry? The swift stab of fence,
barb unraveled. Wires trace frog call across
stale shoal, rest on a forehead at night, tear
the shirt, help drive the single-flue harpoon
into the body, deliver the stake
to sprouted seed. Listen, Kearney, to rain-

drops hitting ground, tie them down
and they vanish instantly. A farmer's song,
the gin drum upon the tired heart, his hat off,
a biscuit's quiet steam, spoon to mouth, dust
blown from nostril, the old American
four-note purr before the first sown crop-dream.

ANTHONY, CLASS OF '92, ON A SUNDAY MORNING

The church is quiet. The city workers,
        orange-vested, have recently placed American flags

into the chests of telephone poles arranged
        down the throat of Merced Street. The church

is quiet due to a wandering congregation,
        conversing, drifting toward the park across

the street, a half block down. Most chat
        softly as a group of retired men, in matching white

shirts, tune instruments in the band stand. No one
        regards the slender man, early-forties, whose baggy

shorts frame bones that lean against a cinderblock wall
        in heavy summer, breathing silent bugs and prayers.

OUR SCHOOL COLORS

Logan, you took your glass eye out for me.
        It wasn't the taking out that I needed

to see, but the pink folds beneath. We
        studied the jurisdiction of concentration

camps together and that was when
        you first told me that you wanted to

die. You spotted twelve four-leaf clovers
        when I sat with you near the football field

during physical education.
        You never wore baseball caps

but you wore one in that coffin. The shotgun
        took away the top of your skull and they

dressed you up, dusted pink blush—light
        as lead—on your heather-gray cheeks.

THE RIVER WITCH

We all live near a shallow branch of the San Joaquin.
        My sister, her husband,

my brothers, their wives.
        We moved five miles

from the farm into four trailers
        surrounded by young oak,

cattails, and the song of frogs almost unbearable
        on summer nights.

The retired stuntman rides his old mule,
        Missy, over to our communal fire pit.

The pop-top cans of Coors
        and the crickets cannot hide

our laughter. He tells us keep it down
        without saying we might wake the River Witch.

I'm sure her howl would not be heard
        over our laughter drowning

in the gathering mist.
        Logs spark up into the black.

I think of a glacier letting go of its shoulders
        to unburden its weight into the sea.

I think of the River Witch, how
        she watches young stupid couples

get themselves all wrapped up in concepts like *family*.
        I think of Seth Kendall and his sister.

They were stupid too; a raft made of reeds
        and life jackets, they too thought they could

get beyond the mundane, the regular, and they did.
        Seth's body was found beneath Trout Bridge

and his sister Glenda, unanchored, was nudged
        by a houseboat on Sycamore Lake. The passengers

thought she was driftwood. We know this is not
        our fate. We sing *kumbyya my lord* and try

not to think of the pieces of John's skull on Jackie's coat.
        We are young and have everything

figured out. Our divorces, the end of the Vietnam War,
        our friends, and *Missy*, not yet gone.

RIDE THE 28 ACROSS THE RIVER STYX

Someone has drawn tulips with a black sharpie
        on the plastic frame of the bus seat. A woman

seated there with *DEAD* tattooed in block letters
        on her neck teases strands of her man's russet

hair. Ringlets stir against his shoulders below
        a backward *A's* ball cap. The bus stops, I exit

toward a hearse gracelessly parked. Its driver
        leans against it, pinching a cigarette, smiling.

LISTENING TO NINA SIMONE SING *SINNERMAN*

for William Edward Anderson

A bird sets its silhouette behind white sheets
        on a clothesline that belongs to a half-collapsed
                neighboring house; a house that never comes

alive. On days when wind pulls heat off roads
        and sends it down vineyards outside town,
                the house, still, never comes alive. Although

today, after news of a friend's death, I hear
        an old familiar song freed from our neighbor's
                screened porch; I see the bleeding river, boiling

sea, the sharpest gospel sting, poplar dust, ascent
        of magnolia blossom, the rush of air between
                the sides of each dried sheet, the pale light

of August sun burning the last drops of water
        in a hose near a black-red mulberry stain. The
                berry must have dropped and burst in June—

sealed its mark—an angel with wings spread
        on concrete. When a friend dies, we think about
                making appointments with the doctor; we dream

x-rays, white hospital linens, beeps and blood
        stains—we repeatedly recite the simplest lyric:
                so I run to the lord, please hide me lord.

HARDPAN

> *And the dead tree gives no shelter, the cricket no relief,*
> *And the dry stone no sound of water*
>   —T.S. Eliot, The Burial of the Dead

The sparse rain and extant sun trick the crepe myrtle.
Pink clouds burst along the dry branch, blushing
despite brittle soil and bending weeds.

Snow keeps roots dormant, blanketed for sleep,
waiting to wake at the onset of another harsh season.
Every year, when spring has gone and the heat tumbles

down the Sierras, we enjoy the brief showers
that stave the blazing heft and glimmering sunlight.
How easily we talk on afternoons like this at the café.

We recall the white afternoons at my Uncle's farm.
How my cousin buried me in snow. You laughed, then.
You said, "We will not leave you there,

keep still." And so I, trustingly, slept in snow.
Still, we meet here in the summer and meet there in winter.
Summer is cruel and steals water. Insects do not sing

and the creeks back away. We have air-conditioning,
swimming pools, water from faucets.
I will show you fear in a handful of dust.

All that remains is sameness. We are comfortable.
Our shadows follow us, the dust settles. We hide.
In the evenings we sleep, having bound our shadows

to the retreating sun. *Fresh blows the wind.*
The home of my childhood. Where are you now?
You are always the same, snow-flaked,

sun-lit, or otherwise. Last year, we visited Madame Sophia,
in Fowler, just off Highway 99. You told me she could see
further into someone than any other diviner. The drowned

Phoenician Sailor was the first card she pulled for you
(death by water, eyes like tide-pools, cloudy pearls).
Belladonna was pulled next, St. John the Baptist and Christ

brought together. The Wheel. The Hanged Man. These
cards appeared in succession. An audience to you,
the parts of me that know you, a sermon to the choir.

Harsh Valley, mother of tule fog that holds the water, vaporous,
in the air, keeps the moisture above ground.
There is a constant holding-back, a tease that teaches

survival to the agriculture that thrives here. Winter,
that cruel hypnotist. Spring, the trickster; Summer, the oppressor.
It is on the hottest day, after our meeting,

that we bring out the shovels, and the hose, to plant
another tree in the foothills near my Uncle's farm.
This is the most difficult time to do so.

Heat, drought, dogs that dig, hardpan at the tips
of the roots. We live in it, we are buried here,
still breathing, and nothing stops us.

V.

PORTRAIT OF A POEM IN SUMMER

This poem descends from the sky—

a plastic bag, a hat. Its hull
        becomes a flea market. It fries trout

in a cast iron pan. It is San Joaquin
        summer when the crepe myrtle weeps.

It is the culled grape leaf, blood
        let from thorn, the dust entering,

oil leaked. It holds the young tree
        by its small trunk, lets mist live

in brown hair—releases itself
        from ocean, creek, and canal.

CORAL SCRAPES HIS BACK

and blood reaches out
        in clouds, curling slowly

down, slowly down, past
        a damselfish into the giant

clam whose lips stay open
        for my hand. The man

above is big; big and white,
        a back of cod opened up,

blossoming. I stay down,
        looking. The cool weight

sits on my chest; clam's
        mouth closes. All white

and red, white, red, white,
        and blue and the sun cuts

all the shapes apart. See
        the clam's mouth silent;

turn to hear parrotfish
        chewing branches; see

eye of humphead wrasse.
        The figure lifts from red

shadows before the sharks
        come. No

white-tipped reef shark,
        not one hammerhead.

THOUGH THE EARTH BE MOVED

to those lost in the 1964 Alaskan Earthquake

Orange light streams through the faux wood
Venetians, spreads rivers across the television
and the coffee table, reflects off the green
Ticonderoga embossed across the yellow shaft
of my pencil. I write them down: *Passaic Falls,
Sutro Baths, Bowery Waltz, Capsize of Lifeboat,
An Arrest in Chinatown, 40 seconds of Monterey
Surf*; all Edison films, 1890s. These films, saved
by the Library of Congress, are flat as ice, they
roll across the computer screen as my fingers
trace, leaving trails of light—aurora borealis
echoing above html. I see the ocean folding
itself, lifting, dropping, lifting and dropping.
I see the men walk across the ice, drift out,
fold into breakers; I hear nothing. Memories
fold into themselves. A bridge swallows a car.
Earthquakes shake Wasco, Shafter, Weedpatch,
Frazier Park, and Buttonwillow, shiver the ten
foot windows of my wife's classroom twice
in one week—the glass could shatter; she could
be swallowed; the splitting of molecules could split
hers, but I fight this thought as I see our lives
divining by the light through Venetian blinds.

FOUND PHOTO FROM A GRADUATION

The tops of trees sit at the raw-hide-brown
        foot of an overcast sky. The shapes change

heft, cradle to groan, cradle to crack, blurred,
        dim, scratched. The school colors—yellow,

white—strike low light. The graduates align.
        Blue draped men, women in white. Light

pushes toward deep copper shafts, mist-gray
        sheets. Telephone pole is covered with deep

green ivy. The piled clouds are less gray. One
        blurred face looks out from the row of gowns;

beneath the white and blue, the red dust
        frames a setting sun, centered—diffused.

ON THURSDAY MORNING, THE ROAD WAKES TO THE WHEELS OF GARBAGE MEN

The road that leads out of this town is thin;
it traverses full canals on its way toward other
small towns. On Thursday morning, when

the garbage truck heaves its load into its back,
August air pauses, stills all objects. Trucks,
loaded with waste, tractor equipment or fruit,

press on the hot asphalt and, here, in this room,
I feel the foundation vibrate with engine strain,
flare of brake, the weight of mechanical grasp.

At this moment, the mailman drops coupons
through our slot; he walks off, over dry lawn,
steps on the spot where a mockingbird pulled

worm from earth the day before—I watched
from the dining room, sun inching in, coffee hot
as August. Thursday mornings, like this,

are glistening with barberry thorn. Curled arms
of stinging fern collect light on each margin.
Steam catches yellow sun in diminutive bulbs.

Cars carry retired couples to wherever they go
so early, and the road is tired, small, and broken.
It seems, to you, that not much happens here.

You, who sees the same thing every Thursday
morning, traverses each detail so frequently
that canals fill and empty without testimony;

the garbage trucks vibrate your floors weekly,
the empty alleyways fill with light when birds
wake before the hot hours. The schedule keeps.

SUMMER ENDS EACH MORNING

for Vartan

Wake with one slipper under
the sheets, with a shirt on backwards.
Wake again to reject the possibility

of not waking. Give your wife a kiss
on the lips before pulling yourself out
of bed. Kiss her the way a husband

kisses his wife—though sometimes
she is your mother. Hold the wall
beneath your portrait and move one

foot in front of the bare other. You will
not remember your dreams; you will
not remember your breakfast. You do,

however, see the scrub jay perched
on the persimmon tree as you drink
your coffee and await the right season.

PROUD FLESH

for Nancy

As wide as a fang, cruel as a snake,
        the cut, just above the pastern,

is too deep. Keep it clean.
        Her withers sink.

Hooves dig at the young blueweed.
        The pasture is quiet.

Listen to her.
        The blood is hot.

Listen to her.
        The others know

that the stall may remain vacant.
        Slough the new tissue away.

Dark eyes water
        and the throat-latch aches.

WE NAME THE FOX

The fox gathers spiders
from between rose bush thorns,
from beneath the bottom fence-
rail, into her lean jaws. She
is ready to give milk; we name
her *Joyce*. Our girls run
to the east side of the house,
then the west, hunting views.
I call her name and she looks up,
listens, looks between the carport
gate and the black trash bin, she
processes an object divide—
she preens air almost motionlessly.
If I were to define this stillness,
I would do so in silence.

SOMETHING IN THE WALL

I cannot access email and some-
    thing is paddling its way up
        the inside of the wall. Maybe

it's a woodrat, raw pink eyes
    from no light, matted
        fur scratching the nest,

wrestling against the wood-
    paneled walls because it's the first
        fire of the season and the flue

is hot, damper open, cool air
    pulling the heat up and up. This
        fireplace, that has not been used

in over two years, the displaced
    creature, emails lost in the sky,
        our home's changing body,

all this, cause for concern. Perhaps
    I haven't rigged the proper fire-
        wire—whatever that is—therefore

the web is unstable, like our old dog,
    who stared and stirred, who couldn't
        hear the scurrying and would not care.

THE CARBON FOOTPRINT OF A RATTLESNAKE

My mother, stepbrother, stepfather, raise
tents at the low camp by the slow-lapping

wakes of Pine Flat Lake. Anchor holds the small
aluminum boat close, its shell thumping

quiet against the mud. Speedboat engines echo
the coves; we do not see them. I'm thinking

about the creek at Mineral King where
orange salamanders once leapt across my

six-year-old fingers. I sit, sweating,
on the shore. My little brother wades out,

water soaks his diaper, his little hands
slap the silt clouds. The dim mountains shudder

at the jolt of a gunshot; we look back.
My stepfather holds the headless rattler;

its thick body tightens in a death curl.
The fire is stoked and though the coals

are not yet red, and the sun has not set,
the long body is skinned, gutted, and

splayed out. The tips of ribs blacken; neck
opens wide its mouth, light pink—almost white—

charcoal kissed, darkening. Moisture rises
to the surface of each muscle's thread. Cold

blood hot now. The day rolls over. Poisons,
tiny needle bones, pull from the small body.

There is something about the smell of burnt
meat, black pepper, gasoline in lake water.

LOGIC

for John Berryman

The stone fruit; the brown shirt—
the sun rises and sets, and not all

men's shirts have a horizontal
buttonhole to end the homogenous

line. Not all. I pick a nectarine
from a leaning branch and avoid

the one bitten by an animal other
than myself. The stone fruit with

intact skin, the predictable choice;
the brown shirt—of conservative

design, decisive turn. The sun will
rise at morning, set before night.

WAKING TO WATCH ACCIDENTS ON YOUTUBE

I turn it off after five minutes; that
is a lie. I keep it on to keep eye
on the cop falling over a fence, the land

rover mowing down motorcyclists,
the sun-blind captain falling between
two boats. I think about the starlings—

a twenty-minute drive away—screaming
across the Costco parking lot and I stay.
I stay to watch a fake megalodon nudge

a great white shark, a baby who trips over
and over and over a Tonka truck to end up
headfirst in a pond of white ducklings. I stop

to eat yogurt, drink coffee outside, watch
our old dog piss on the frost, stop,
in my robe, to contemplate returning

to the search engine to type "Great Poets
in Their Own Words" to redeem and watch
W.H. Auden spill a thousand drinks down

the front of his shirt, to stifle and keep
my mouth from swallowing itself as Anne
Sexton falls down a flight of stairs, laughing.

TOO MANY CROWS IN CLOVIS, CA

They do not block the sun; they scatter
dust light and shadows onto my forehead
as I drive to the end of Highway 168

toward houses that wait, half-built, hiding
seedless orchards in their basements. I park
across from a truck marked Dreamscape Pools,

ignore the slow dirge of the cement mixer,
and walk to the front door, entering
with a key that sometimes works.

He's in his robe, half-open, knees naked
beneath the table, his brown leather belt
wrapped around his waist.

She's already dressed in her powder blue
sweatsuit, hair done, newspaper
out, checking the obituaries.

They eat their toasted raisin bread with
Armenian string cheese, pills, and cantaloupe.
My grandfather asks my grandmother

who I am. I pour him more coffee
and ask, *Who am I?* He says,
I don't know.

I say, *Yes you do* and smile. He stares at me…
Ronnie? I answer *Yessir*. He asks,
Who is your father?

You know who he is. Who is my father?
He pauses, looks into himself… *Steve?*
and I say, *Yessir. So what does that make me?*

He looks at his wife, who shakes her head in her hands,

looks back, *Are you my grandson?*
Yes I am. Does that surprise you?

He comes to the cliff of almost-tears and stops,
Oh no, that makes me very happy. What a small world.
He and my grandmother touch hands, smile, he forgets.

I clean their empty plates, wash my hands,
fold the kitchen towel, put the coffee pot away.
And once they are asleep in front of the television,

I kiss them each, once, on their foreheads,
tell them that I will see them in two days.
I lock the door behind me, walk

toward my car, move through
song of nailgun and bulldozer.
I do not look at the crows.

DEER AND SNOW IN LAKEVIEW, OR

    for Vartan

A plot of tall grass stands in the small town,
tallest in Oregon, between the gas
station and the clapboard realty office.

After we've filled the tank, perused thrift
stores across North 1st Street, my family
and I look at the lot, it looks back—six

sets of eyes, deer, sole citizens of this
vacancy. I tell you this through time-slips,
grandfather, since you cannot watch with us

from this wet asphalt where we hear snow
melt in trees; you will not catch the young light
in eyes of buck in a town that will not

be home. We are passing, new water through
western hemlock, steam through teeth in the mild
stillness of slow passing cars and storm air.

We pass between the eyelashes of our children
and—among the letters with which I form
these words—the emptiness remains in white.

Ronald Dzerigian earned his M.F.A. in poetry from California State University, Fresno. He resides in a small farming community with his wife and two daughters.

www.ingramcontent.com/pod-product-compliance
Lightning Source LLC
Chambersburg PA
CBHW070550090426
42735CB00013B/3131